Béisbol! Latino Heroes of Major League Baseball

MIGUEL Cabrera

JOSH LEVENTHAL

BLACK
RABBIT
BOOKS

Bolt is published by Black Rabbit Books
P.O. Box 3263, Mankato, Minnesota, 56002.
www.blackrabbitbooks.com
Copyright © 2017 Black Rabbit Books

Design and Production by Michael Sellner
Photo Research by Rhonda Milbrett

Library of Congress Control Number: 2015954917

HC ISBN: 978-1-68072-045-7   PB ISBN: 978-1-68072-303-8

Printed in the United States at CG Book Printers,
North Mankato, Minnesota, 56003. PO #1797 4/16

Web addresses included in this book were working and appropriate
at the time of publication. The publisher is not responsible for broken
or changed links.

Contents

4

CHAPTER 1

A Latino Legend

Rookie Miguel Cabrera steps up to the plate. It's the bottom of the 11th inning. There is one out. Cabrera smashes the first pitch deep to center field. It's a game-winning home run!

Fantastic Hitter • • • • • • • • • •

Cabrera is an all-star player. He is one of the best hitters in baseball. He plays hard in the field too. Some people even call him one of the greatest players in baseball.

Cabrera grew up in Venezuela. Baseball was in his blood. His father played **amateur** baseball. His mother was on the national softball team.

Venezuela

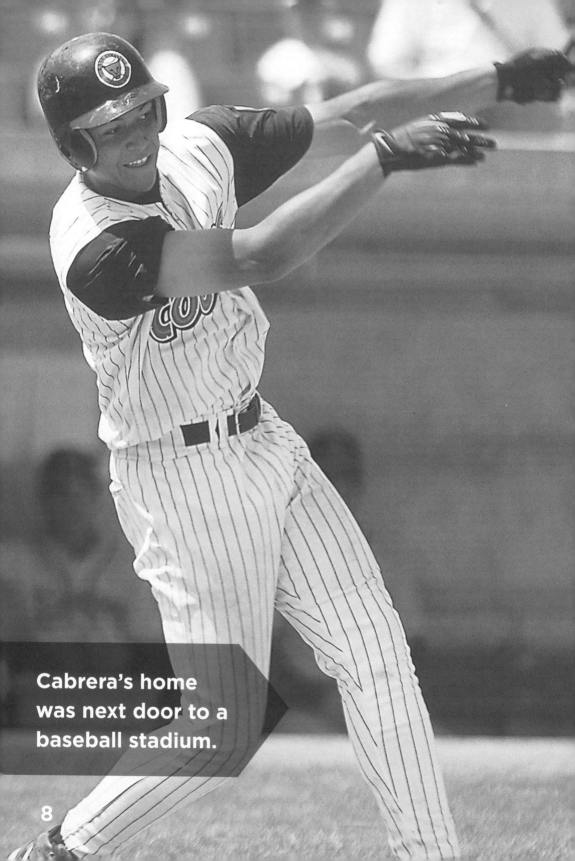

Cabrera's home was next door to a baseball stadium.

CHAPTER 2

A Young Baseball Star

Cabrera was born April 18, 1983. Young Cabrera was an excellent hitter. He was also a good fielder. He could play the infield and outfield.

Major League Baseball (MLB) **scouts** watched him play as a teenager. The Marlins signed him to a contract in 1999.

The Minor Leagues

Cabrera played in the **minor leagues** for just over three years. In 2003, he hit 10 homers in 69 games. The Marlins knew Cabrera was ready. They called him up to the major leagues.

A batting average shows how often a player gets a hit. An average of .300 is excellent.

Fun Facts

right
handed

WEIGHT

240
POUNDS
(109 kilograms)

6 feet
4 inches (1.9 m)
tall

6'

5'

4'

He earns about
$30 million
a year.

He started
a group to
raise money
for students.
It also fixes
baseball
fields.

nickname
is Miggy

CHAPTER 3

In the

Majors

Cabrera hit a home run in his first MLB game. He got base hits in five of his first six games. Cabrera was named **National League** Rookie of the Month twice. It was an excellent start for the rookie.

Games Cabrera Played in Each Position (2003-2015)

1st base
831

3rd base
696

left
field
248

right
field
100

15

World Series

Cabrera helped his team get to the World Series in 2003. He hit three homers in the Championship Series.

He had three **runs batted in** (RBI) during the World Series. He tied for the most on the team. Nobody expected the Marlins to beat the Yankees. But they did.

All-Star Regular

Cabrera was an All-Star every year from 2004 to 2007. He led the Marlins in RBIs each of those years. He also led the team in home runs in three years.

Consecutive Seasons with 100 or More RBIs

through 2015

Five players in history have 100 RBIs in more than 10 straight seasons.

Lou Gehrig
(1926–1938)

13

Jimmie Foxx
(1929–1941)

13

Alex Rodriguez
(1998–2010)

13

Al Simmons
(1924–1934)

11

Miguel Cabrera
(2004–2014)

11

.400
.350
.300
.250
.200
.150

| .268 | .294 | .323 | .339 | .320 | .292 |
| 2003 | 2004 | 2005 | 2006 | 2007 | 2008 |

Traded

After the 2007 season, the Marlins traded Cabrera. He went to the Tigers. He led the American League (AL) with 37 homers in 2008. His .344 average in 2011 was best in the league. Cabrera was becoming one of the best hitters in baseball.

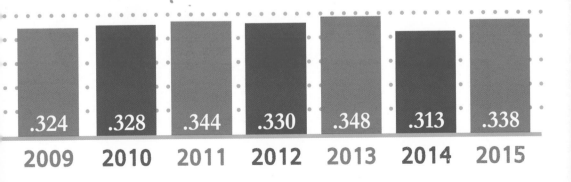

Cabrera's Yearly MLB Batting Averages

2009	2010	2011	2012	2013	2014	2015
.324	.328	.344	.330	.348	.313	.338

CHAPTER 4

Continuing to Impress

In 2012, Cabrera won the Triple Crown. He was the first player in 45 years to do that. He was also named the AL Most Valuable Player (MVP). He also won MVP the next year.

139

led the league in RBIs

Cabrera's **Triple Crown**

.330

had the league's highest batting average

44

led the AL in home runs

CABRERA'S MLB CAREER STATISTICS

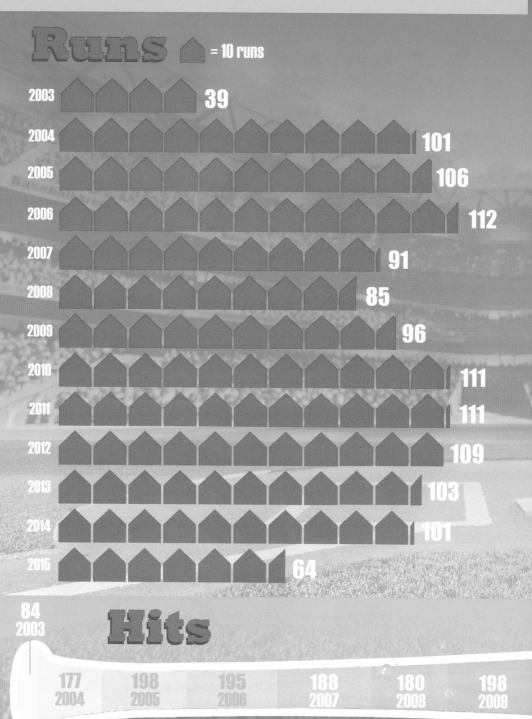

Runs ⌂ = 10 runs

Year	Runs
2003	39
2004	101
2005	106
2006	112
2007	91
2008	85
2009	96
2010	111
2011	111
2012	109
2013	103
2014	101
2015	64

Hits

| 84 2003 | 177 2004 | 198 2005 | 195 2006 | 188 2007 | 180 2008 | 198 2009 |

Games Played

2003	87	2006	158	2009	160	2012	161
2004	160	2007	157	2010	150	2013	148
2005	158	2008	160	2011	161	2014	159
						2015	119

Home Runs

12	33	33	26	34	37	34
2003	2004	2005	2006	2007	2008	2009

38	30	44	44	25	18
2010	2011	2012	2013	2014	2015

Runs Batted In

2003	2004	2005	2006	2007	2008	2009	2010	2011	2012	2013	2014	2015
62	112	116	114	119	127	103	126	105	139	137	109	76

180	197	205	193	191	145
2010	2011	2012	2013	2014	2015

Powerful Player

Cabrera is one of the best players in baseball today. He has more than 400 career homers. His .338 average in 2015 was the best in the league. Fans can't wait to see what he does next.

Cabrera's Awards (through 2015)

2 MVPs

10 ALL-STAR GAMES

6 SILVER SLUGGERS

Timeline

1983

April

Cabrera is born.

1999

signs with the Marlins

2003

October

Marlins win World Series

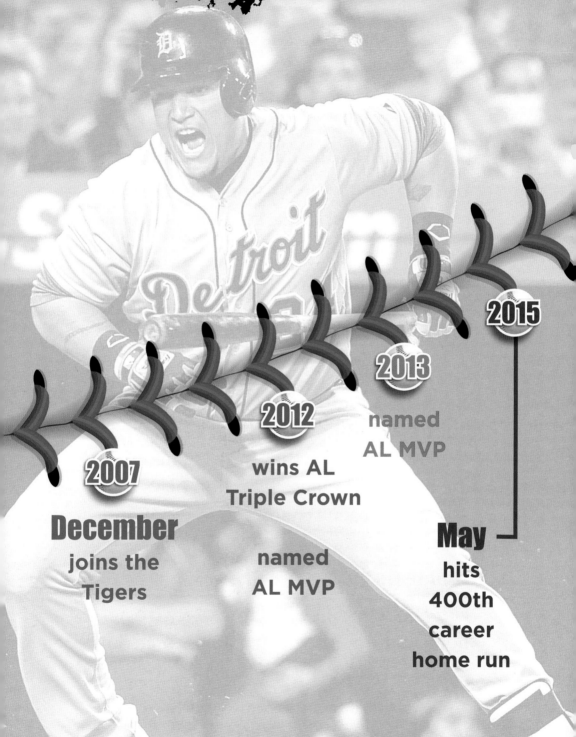

2007

December
joins the
Tigers

2012

wins AL
Triple Crown

named
AL MVP

2013

named
AL MVP

2015

May
hits
400th
career
home run

amateur (AM-uh-chur)—not professional

Latino (luh-TEE-no)—from Mexico or a country in South America, Central America, or the Caribbean

minor league (MY-nur LEEG)— a professional baseball organization that competes at levels below the major leagues

National League (NAH-shun-uhl LEEG)— one of two groups that make up Major League Baseball in the United States; the National League champion plays the American League champion in the World Series each year.

rookie (ROOK-ee)—a first-year player

run (RUN)—when a player safely crosses home plate before the team has three outs

runs batted in (RUNZ BAT-ud IN)—when a player's at-bat causes one or more players to score a run

scout (SKOWT)—a person sent to get information about someone or something

BOOKS

Anderson, Jameson. *Miguel Cabrera*. Awesome Athletes. Minneapolis: ABDO Pub. Company, 2015.

Mattern, Joanne. *Miguel Cabrera*. A Robbie Reader. Hockessin, DE: Mitchell Lane Publishers, 2014.

Rauf, Don. *Miguel Cabrera: Triple Crown Winner*. Living Legends of Sports. New York: Britannica Educational Publishing in association with Rosen Educational Services, 2016.

WEBSITES

Baseball
www.ducksters.com/sports/baseball.php

Miguel Cabrera
m.mlb.com/player/408234/miguel-cabrera

Miguel Cabrera
www.miggy24.com

INDEX